TAPAS

And More Great Dishes from Spain

By Janet Mendel

Photography by John James Wood

Published in Spain by
SANTANA BOOKS
Apartado 422,
29640 Fuengirola, Málaga.
Tel. (95) 248 5838. Fax (95) 248 5367.
e-mail: santana@vnet.es

Food preparation and styling
by Janet Mendel and Jacqueline Lescott
Acknowledgements: Many thanks to the following who provided props,
locations and assistance: Charlotte Gordon, Paffard Keating-Clay,
Antonio Moledo, Audrey Pannell, Jan Volz.
Designed by Gregson Design Tel: (95) 277 54 66
Printed in Spain by Gráficas San Pancracio S.L.,
Calle Orotava 17, Polg. Ind. San Luis, Málaga.

ISBN: 84-89954-01-1. Depósito Legal: MA-1.190/1997

Table of Contents

TAPAS
And More Great Dishes From Spain
An Introduction to Spanish Cooking

Spain's cooking is quintessentially Mediterranean—the sunny flavours of olive oil, fresh fruits and vegetables, seafood and wine. But its styles and flavours vary considerably by region, for Spain is a large country.

Compared to the cuisines of neighbouring France and Italy, Spanish food seems more exotic, due to the influence of the Moors (Muslims from Arabia and North Africa), who occupied Spain for many centuries, right up until 1492, when the last Moorish stronghold, the Alhambra of Granada, was defeated by the troops of King Ferdinand and Queen Isabella.

The Moorish heritage shows up in the use of ground almonds and spices such as saffron, cinnamon, nutmeg and sesame, even in savoury dishes; in the love of rice dishes such as paella, (the Moors introduced rice-growing to Spain); and in the honeyed sweets and pastries. Even today, you will find similarities between Spanish food and the cuisine of nearby Morocco, just across the Strait of Gibraltar.

But, also many differences. For one, Spanish cooking includes the wide use of pork, ham and sausage, which, of course, is forbidden in the Muslim diet. More importantly, after Columbus set sail from Spain and discovered a New World, Spain in the 15th and 16th centuries became a world power, exploring and colonising three continents. The Spanish conquistadores didn't just discover gold—they discovered new foods, such as tomatoes, potatoes and maize, chocolate, beans and squash, peppers, pineapple and avocados, which eventually enriched Spanish and European diets.

Don't expect Spanish cooking to be like Mexican or Hispanic food. While the Hispanic countries of the Americas share some of the dishes from colonial Spain, Spain's own cooking is nothing at all like the indigenous Indian cooking of the Americas—no corn tortillas, no hot-hot chili. No "salsa!"

So, what 's Spanish? Best-known dishes are *paella*, saffron-rice with chicken and seafood, typical of the eastern regions of Spain where rice is grown; *gazpacho*, a cold soup of raw ingredients from Andalusia in southern Spain; *fabada* a hearty bean and sausage casserole from Asturias in the north; *romesco*, a fabulous sauce of sweet peppers and crushed nuts, which the Catalans serve with grilled fish; *cocido*, a meal-in-a-pot, typical of the capital, Madrid, but, in fact, served in every region of the country, and *tortilla*, which in Spain is a fat round potato and egg omelette. Add to that list superb seafood dishes from all the coastal regions—Spain consumes more fish and shellfish than any other European country— plus an enticing array of sweets.

Spanish products appreciated abroad include fine olives, particularly the Seville manzanillas; capers; oranges; avocados; saffron; dried figs and raisins; almonds and other nuts; cured *serrano* ham; canned shellfish.

You can create authentic Spanish food in your own kitchen, with ingredients easy to find in local shops. The selection of recipes in this book includes of few of Spain's exotic dishes—for example, squid in its own ink—plus lots more which are easy to prepare, easy to enjoy, with ingredients right at hand. At the back of the book is a useful list of ingredients and utensils.

Que aproveche! Enjoy. Take advantage of Spain's great culinary heritage.

A note about the recipes: For the convenience of cooks on several continents, measurements for ingredients are given in metric, British imperial measures, and American standard measures. The American measurements appear in parentheses. Where American terminology is different from British, the American word is in parentheses. For example, aubergine (eggplant).

Chapter 1
The Tapas Experience

Just follow the crowds through this doorway, into the cool interior of a typical *bodega* or wine bar. Multi-coloured tiles line the walls, while clay-tiled floors shine with the patina of years of footsteps. Barrels of wine are stacked behind the bar. From wooden beams hang whole hams and links of sausages, ropes of garlic and peppers. You order a glass of wine and the barman asks if you would like a tapa. Tapas are small portions of foods, both hot and cold, served in wine bars and in *tascas*, taverns, to accompany a *copa* of *fino*, dry Spanish Sherry; *vino*, wine; *cava*, sparkling wine; *sidra*, cider, or draught beer. You can enjoy tapas in most bars before the lunch hour (in Spain this is very late—tapas at 1 p.m., lunch at 2 p.m. or after), and again before dinner (7-9 p.m., with dinner later yet). Tapas are a great introduction to Spanish food because you can share a selection of them amongst several friends.

Tapas are served in bars in every region of Spain and every region has its variations on the theme. The word means "cover". In wine-making regions, such as Jerez, home of Sherry, a tiny saucer is customarily placed to cover a glass of wine in order to keep the little fruit flies from swarming in. A titbit of food placed on the dish would help attract clients to the wine bar, so the cook—usually the owner's wife—would out-do herself to make more and better ones. In some bars the tapa is served free with the wine.

Tapa hopping is part of the convivial Spanish way of life. With a few friends you stop in at several bars to have a glass of wine and sample the tapa specialities of each. It is customary to stand up at the bar, but sometimes you sit at a table and order whole rations or plates of food to share.

Here's a tantalising taste of some of the dishes—hot and cold— you might find in a tapa bar in Spain.

Certainly the superb ham, both *serrano*, which just means mountain-cured, and the pricey *iberico*, produced from special pigs which grow sweet on acorns. This salt-cured ham is served raw, very thinly sliced. It makes a marvellous combination with fino Sherry.

Amongst cold dishes on the tapa bar are a variety of salads, some wonderfully exotic. For example, *salpicón* with chopped tomatoes, onions and peppers might include prawns and mussels or it might be made with chopped, cooked octopus. *Remojón* is a salad of oranges, codfish, onions and olives. While it might sound strange, it tastes wonderful.

Spain is famous for its fish and shellfish and a tapa bar is a great place to sample the array. Fried fish, from tiny fresh anchovies (*boquerones*) and rings of tender squid (*calamares*) to chunks of fresh hake and batter-dipped prawns are enticing, indeed. Look for *cazón en adobo*, fish marinated before frying, and *boquerones en vinagre*, marinated raw fish.

Then come a variety of hot dishes. Some are cooked to order—prawns *pil pil*, sizzled with garlic and oil; or garlicky grilled pork loin—while others are dished out of a bubbling stew-pot. You can savour meatballs in almond sauce, kidneys in Sherry sauce, sautéed mushrooms, chicken fried *al ajillo* - with lots and lots of garlic, lamb stew, broad beans with ham, piquant tripe, spicy snails, and, of course, *tortilla*, a thick round potato omelette. Fritters and croquettes, crisp-fried in olive oil, are other great tapas of Spain, which produces the world's finest olive oil.

Tapas are always accompanied by good bread—in chunks for mopping up sauces, sliced to top with ham or cheese, or breadsticks.

Tapas make for great parties. A selection of a few of these dishes is a lively change from canapés, while a lavish spread could serve as a buffet dinner. Most dishes can be prepared in advance, meaning you have only some last-minute preparations and re-heating. Also, many of these tapas can substitute for starters, and, amongst the main courses are several which can be served as tapas. You see how versatile?

Here are a few recipes to get you started.

Spanish Potato Omelette
Tortilla Española

A *tortilla* is a big golden disk, which can be cut into wedges or squares to be served as a tapa. It also makes a nice supper dish.

6 tablespoons olive oil
1 kg /2 lb potatoes, peeled and thinly sliced
2 tablespoons chopped onion
6 eggs
1 teaspoon salt

Heat the oil in a no-stick or well-seasoned frying pan (24-26 cm / 9-10 inches). Add the sliced potatoes and turn them in the oil. Let them cook slowly in the oil, without browning, turning frequently. When they are partially cooked, add the chopped onion. The potatoes will take 20-30 minutes to cook. Beat the eggs in a bowl with the salt. Put a plate over the potatoes and drain off excess oil into another bowl. Add the potatoes to the beaten eggs and combine well. Add a little of the reserved oil to the frying pan and pour in the potato-egg mixture. Cook on a medium heat until set, without letting the omelette get too brown on the bottom, about 5 minutes. Shake the pan to keep the tortilla from sticking. Place a flat lid or plate over the pan, hold it tightly, and reverse the tortilla onto the plate. Add a little more oil to the pan, if necessary, and slide the tortilla back in to cook on the reverse side, about 3 minutes more. Slide out onto a serving plate. Serve hot or cold.

Cut into squares, makes 15-20 appetiser servings, or, sliced, 4 luncheon or supper servings.

Meatballs in Saffron-Almond Sauce
Albóndigas con Salsa de Almendras y Azafrán

This saffron-tinged sauce thickened with crushed almonds makes a nice change on the meatball theme. Saffron is grown in Spain and you can buy it in Spanish markets. If the real spice is not available, substitute ½ teaspoon of paprika or a drop of yellow food colouring.

800 g / 1 ¾ lb minced beef and pork
50 g / 1 ¾ oz (2 slices) stale bread, crusts removed
1 clove garlic, minced
3 tablespoons minced onion
2 tablespoons chopped parsley
½ teaspoon salt
freshly grated nutmeg
2 eggs, beaten
flour
6 tablespoons olive oil
40 almonds, blanched and skinned
25 g / 1 oz (1 slice) bread
3 tablespoons olive oil
10 peppercorns
½ teaspoon saffron
1 clove
½ teaspoon salt
150 ml / ¼ pint (⅔ cup) white wine
250 ml / 9 fl oz (1 cup) meat or chicken stock
lemon juice
chopped parsley

Combine the minced beef and pork in a bowl. Soak the sliced bread in water or milk to cover until soft. Squeeze it out and add to the meat with the garlic, onion, parsley, salt, nutmeg and egg. Knead well to make a smooth mixture. Form into small balls (3 cm / 1 inch). Roll them in flour and fry very slowly in hot oil until browned on all sides. Remove and drain. The oil can be strained and used for the sauce.

Fry the almonds, bread and garlic in the oil until golden. Remove. In a mortar, crush the peppercorns, saffron, clove and salt. Add the toasted almonds, bread and garlic (or put it in a processor) with the wine to make a smooth paste. Combine this mixture in the pan with remaining oil and the stock. Bring to a boil, then add the fried meatballs. Simmer the meatballs for 20 minutes in the sauce, adding a little additional liquid if needed. Immediately before serving, add a squeeze of lemon juice. Serve sprinkled with chopped parsley.

Makes about 36 meatballs.

Marinated Fried Fish
Cazón en Adobo

Many tapa dishes can be prepared well in advance, but those which are fried, like this one, should be served immediately. While in Spain this is usually made with a kind of shark, which benefits from the tangy marinade, any solid-fleshed fish, such as monkfish, works well.

800 g / 1 ¾ lb bone-free fish, such as shark or monkfish
3 tablespoons olive oil
5 tablespoons wine vinegar
1 tablespoon water
3 cloves garlic, chopped
¼ teaspoon paprika
1 teaspoon oregano
¼ teaspoon ground black pepper
½ teaspoon salt
flour
olive oil for frying

Cut the fish into 4-cm/1 ½-inch cubes, discarding any skin and bone. Put it in a glass or ceramic bowl. Mix together the oil, vinegar, water, garlic, paprika, oregano, pepper and salt. Pour over the fish and mix well. Marinate for at least 6 hours or overnight. Then drain the fish well, dredge it in flour and fry the pieces a few at a time in hot oil until golden and crisp. Drain on paper towelling and serve hot.

Makes about 45 pieces.

Shellfish Cocktail
Salpicón de Mariscos

This is an attractive dish to serve for a buffet dinner. Try it also as a first course. In Spanish tapa bars, this salad also is made using chopped cooked octopus instead of the shellfish.

½ kg /1 lb mussels, scrubbed and steamed open
250 g /½ lb peeled prawns (shrimp)
½ kg /1 lb tomatoes, chopped
½ onion, chopped
1 green pepper, chopped
½ cucumber, peeled and chopped (optional)
2 hard-cooked eggs
1 clove garlic, crushed
6 tablespoons extra virgin olive oil
5 tablespoons wine vinegar
3 tablespoons chopped parsley
1 teaspoon salt
lettuce to garnish

Discard mussel shells and any mussels which do not open. If you like, save a few on the half-shell to garnish the platter. Cook the peeled prawns in boiling salted water for 1 minute and drain. In a bowl combine the chopped tomatoes, onion, green pepper, cucumber and chopped egg whites. Mash the yolks with the crushed garlic. Whisk in the olive oil, vinegar, parsley and salt. Add the prawns and mussels to the tomato mixture. Stir in the dressing and chill, covered, until serving time. Serve on a platter garnished with lettuce.

Makes 12 tapa servings or 6 starters.

Catalan Tomato Toasts
Pan amb Tomat

How could anything so simple be so delicious? Maybe it's not so simple—you need really good country bread, superb olive oil and the finest raw *serrano* ham. And, for sure, vine-ripened tomatoes from Spain. While this is a favourite tapa all over Spain, it's also served for breakfast.

day-old bread, thickly sliced
garlic (optional)
ripe tomato

extra virgin olive oil
thinly sliced serrano ham

Toast or grill the slices of bread. Rub one side of each slice with a cut clove of garlic, if desired. Then scrub the toasted bread with a cut tomato. Some people prefer to skin and seed the tomato, then chop it into pulp. One way or another, you want to impregnate the toasted bread with tomato pulp. Drizzle on lots of olive oil. Top with the sliced ham.

15

Roasted Pepper Salad
Ensalada de Pimientos Asados

Sometimes you can buy these roasted peppers at a *panadería*, a bread oven, where they are roasted in the residual heat after the day's bread has baked. Their smoky-sweet fragrance wafts through a whole barrio. This salad is good as a tapa, as a starter or as a side dish with grilled meat, chicken or fish. Should you have any left, purée it in a blender with a little liquid or cream and serve as a sauce. You can make it with all red capsicum (bell) peppers or, for a combination of flavour and colour, red, green and yellow peppers.

6-8 capsicum (bell) peppers, red and/or green and yellow
1 clove garlic, minced
3 tablespoons olive oil
3 tablespoons vinegar
salt and pepper

Roast the peppers over a gas flame, on the barbecue or under the grill (broiler), turning them frequently until charred on all sides. Remove them to a bowl and cover until they are cool enough to handle. Peel off the skin from the peppers. Cut out the stems and seeds and discard them. Tear or cut the peppers into strips and put on a serving plate. Add the minced garlic, oil, vinegar, salt and pepper. Toss gently. Can be prepared in advance and chilled, but serve the salad at room temperature.

Chicken Sizzled with Garlic
Pollo al Ajillo

Aficionados of this dish insist on LOTS of garlic, but disagree as to whether the garlic should be peeled, chopped and fried, or whether whole cloves of garlic should cook with the chicken. While the tapa bar version usually consists of chicken hacked into small bits, this interpretation of the classic calls for chicken wing joints, which cook quickly, but avoid nasty bone splinters. If you're cooking it as a main course dish, use a jointed chicken, but allow longer cooking time and more liquid.

Incidentally, this dish is also made with rabbit.

1 dozen chicken wings, jointed, and wing-tips discarded
6 tablespoons olive oil
10 cloves garlic
1 bay leaf
150 ml / ¼ pint (¾ cup) Sherry, dry or medium
salt and pepper
chopped parsley

Lightly smash the garlic cloves to split the skins. Set aside 5 of them, unpeeled. Peel the remaining cloves and slice them. Heat the oil in a deep frying pan. Add the sliced garlic and sauté just until golden, then skim it out and reserve. Add the chicken pieces to the oil and fry them slowly, adding the unpeeled cloves of garlic. When chicken is browned, add the bay leaf and Sherry, salt and pepper. Continue cooking until liquid is nearly absorbed and the chicken begins to sizzle again. Serve immediately garnished with chopped parsley and the reserved sautéed garlic bits.

Makes 24 pieces.

Country-Style Potato Salad
Ensalada Campera

Any *tapa* bar worth its salt serves up three, four, five or more different salad combinations (which, incidentally, can all be prepared in advance). This one is always a favourite. You'll enjoy it because it's a good variation on old-fashioned potato salad. Lemon juice makes it special.

1 kg /2 lb potatoes
1 teaspoon salt
4 spring onions or 1 small onion, minced
2 medium tomatoes, peeled and chopped
4 tablespoons olive oil
4 tablespoons lemon juice
2 tablespoons chopped parsley
2 hard-cooked eggs, sliced
1 small tin tuna, drained
12 pitted green olives
lettuce

Cook the potatoes in their skins in boiling water until just tender. Drain and chill them. Then peel and slice the potatoes. Combine the salt, minced onion, chopped tomatoes, olive oil, lemon juice and chopped parsley. Combine the potatoes with the dressing. Serve the potato salad spread on a platter with sliced egg, pieces of tuna and olives. Garnish the platter with lettuce leaves.

Serves 10-12 as a tapa or 6 as a side dish.

Grilled Prawns With Romesco Sauce
Langostinos a la Plancha con Salsa de Romesco

Romesco is a Catalan sauce which is truly sensational, particularly with grilled fish and shellfish, but it can accompany any grilled meat or poultry or, thinned with a bit of water, serve as a dressing for vegetables or salads. The sauce is named for a type of dried sweet red pepper, which gives it a characteristic ruddy colour. North Americans have several similar peppers (not hot chilis). Otherwise, substitute an extra spoonful of paprika.

large, unpeeled prawns (jumbo shrimp)
4-5 small dried sweet red peppers
   or 2 tablespoons paprika
1 chili pepper or to taste
3 tomatoes
1 head of garlic
1 dozen almonds, blanched and peeled
2 dozen hazelnuts, skinned
1 slice bread, toasted
1 tablespoon parsley
150 ml / ¼ pint (⅔ cup) olive oil
1 teaspoon salt
1 tablespoon vinegar
freshly ground black pepper

If using the dried peppers, remove stems and seeds and either toast and grind them or else soak in boiling water and scrape the pulp from the skins. Do the same with the chili. Roast the tomatoes and garlic in a hot oven until the tomato skins split, about 15 minutes. Remove. Skin the tomatoes, cut them in half and remove seeds. Skin all the garlic cloves. Put the peppers (or paprika) in a processor with the tomatoes, garlic, almonds, hazelnuts, bread, parsley and part of the olive oil. Process until you have a smooth purée. Beat in remaining oil, salt, vinegar and pepper. The sauce should be the consistency of thick cream. If too thick, thin with a little water or white wine. The romesco sauce can be made in advance. Bring it to room temperature before serving.

Grill the prawns on a hot griddle which has been brushed with oil and sprinkled with coarse salt. They need only 2-3 minutes on each side, depending on size. Serve accompanied by the sauce —and finger bowls for after peeling the prawns. To make a meal of it, prepare a mixed grill of prawns, fish fillets, clams and mussels.

Makes 300 ml / ½ pint of sauce, enough to accompany 3-4 dozen prawns.

Sizzling Prawns
Gambas al Pil Pil

In tapa bars, this is usually prepared in individual ramekins. Take care you don't burn your tongue! These prawns really are sizzling.

For 1 individual serving:
3 tablespoons olive oil
1 clove garlic, sliced
1 piece of chili pepper
10 peeled raw prawns
pinch of paprika
bread

Put the oil, garlic and chili in a small flameproof ramekin. Put it on the heat until oil is quite hot. Add the prawns and paprika and cook just until the prawns turn pink and curl slightly. Serve immediately, while still sizzling, accompanied by bread.

Galician Pork Pie
Empanada Gallega

In Galicia, which is in the northwest corner of Spain, these huge pies are filled with all manner of ingredients—meat, chicken, fish, clams, scallops. A great snack —and also perfect fare for a picnic in the country.

For the dough:
40 g / 1 ½ oz fresh yeast
150 ml / ¼ pint (¾ cup) very warm water
1 teaspoon sugar
500 g / 1 lb (3 ¾ cups) bread flour,
    plus additional for board
1 teaspoon salt
6 tablespoons olive oil
1 egg, beaten

Dissolve the yeast in the water. Beat in the sugar and 3 tablespoons of the flour. Put the yeast mixture in a warm, draft-free place for 15 minutes, or until very bubbly. Place the remaining flour in a large bowl and add the salt. Make a well in the centre and pour in the oil and egg. Then add the yeast mixture. Gradually work the flour into the liquid ingredients. Turn out on a board and knead the dough, for at least 5 minutes, until it is smooth and shiny. Put it in an oiled bowl, turning to coat both sides with oil. Cover with a dampened kitchen towel and place in a warm place to rise. The dough should double in bulk, about 1 hour.

For the filling and baking:
350 g / ¾ lb thinly sliced pork loin
4 tablespoons olive oil
½ teaspoon paprika
1 teaspoon salt
2 onions, chopped
3 cloves garlic, chopped
3 tomatoes, peeled and chopped
1 tablespoon chopped parsley
1 teaspoon oregano
salt and pepper
150 ml / ¼ pint (⅔ cup) white wine
1 small tin red pimientos, drained and cut in strips
2 hard-cooked eggs, sliced
1 egg, beaten

Fry the pork slices in half the oil and set them aside on a plate. Sprinkle them with paprika and salt. Add the remaining oil to the pan and in it fry the chopped onions and garlic until softened. Add the tomatoes, and fry until they are reduced to a sauce. Add the oregano, salt and pepper and wine. Cook until sauce is reduced, about 15 minutes.

Divide the raised dough in half. Keep one half covered. Roll the other half out to a diameter of 30 cm / 12 inches. It will have a thickness of about 1 cm / ⅓ inch. Fit it into a large pie tin. (Or, shape the dough into a rectangle and fit it into a large oven tin.) Spread the dough with half the prepared tomato sauce. Arrange the slices of pork on top, then strips of pimiento and sliced egg. Cover with remaining sauce. Roll out remaining dough and cover the pie. Trim excess dough around the edges and crimp the edges together. Use the trimmings to roll into thin cords and decorate the top of the pie. Cut a steam vent in the centre. Paint the dough with beaten egg. Bake the pie in a preheated hot oven until golden on top, about 35 minutes. Serve hot or cold.

Serves 8.

Peppers Stuffed With Fish
Pimientos de Piquillo Rellenos con Pescado

This turns up in the trendiest tapa bars in Madrid and the Basque Country, and also as a starter in many restaurants. *Piquillo* peppers are a special Spanish red pepper, small, sweet and slightly piquant, with pointed tips. In Spain, you can buy them in tins, already skinned and ready for stuffing. If piquillo peppers are not available, use very small red capsicum (bell) peppers, roasted and peeled (for how-to, see the recipe for Roasted Pepper Salad pg 16).

2 tins piquillo peppers, each 185 g /6 ½ oz
   (about 15 small peppers)
200 g / 7 oz salt cod (*bacalao*), soaked for 24 hours,
   or any cooked white fish
3 cloves garlic, chopped
1 tablespoon onion, minced
2 tablespoons olive oil
1 ½ tablespoons flour
200 ml /7 fl oz (¾ cup + 1 tablespoon) milk
salt and pepper to taste
grating of nutmeg
150 ml /¼ pint (⅔ cup) cream
pinch of cayenne
1 teaspoon vinegar

Drain the tinned piquillo peppers. Allow 6-10 for stuffing and reserve the remainder for the sauce. Shred or flake the soaked codfish or cooked white fish, discarding any skin or bone. In a saucepan, sauté the chopped garlic and onion in the oil until softened. Add the fish, then the flour and cook for 2 minutes. Then whisk in the milk. Season with salt and pepper and nutmeg. Cook, stirring constantly, until the fish mixture is thickened. Remove from heat. Stuff the piquillo peppers with the fish mixture and place them in an oiled baking dish. Bake in a medium-hot oven for 5 minutes. (Alternatively, the peppers may be dusted with flour, then dipped in beaten egg and fried in olive oil, turning them to brown on all sides.)

Meanwhile, purée the remaining peppers in a blender with the cream, cayenne and vinegar. Spoon the sauce onto 6 dishes and place 1 or 2 of the stuffed peppers on each.

Serves 6.

Roasted Vegetables
Escalivada

This is a delicious Catalan way with vegetables. You can roast them on the barbecue or under the grill (broiler). Serve as a tapa, starter, salad, or a side dish with grilled meat or chicken.

2 medium aubergines (eggplant)
2-3 red and green peppers
1 onion
1 head of garlic (optional)
1 tomato
3 tablespoons olive oil
1 tablespoon vinegar
1 teaspoon salt
1 tablespoon chopped parsley

Prick the aubergines all over. Place them on a rack over coals or under grill (broiler) with the peppers, onion, garlic and tomato. (Divide in two batches, if necessary.) Roast the vegetables, turning, until the skins are blackened on all sides. Remove the tomato when the skin splits. Let all the vegetables sit, covered, until cool enough to handle. Then rub or peel off the skins. Tear the aubergine flesh into strips. Remove stems and seeds from peppers and tear into strips. Cut the onion into thin wedges. Sliver some or all of the garlic cloves. Cut the tomato into wedges. Combine all the vegetables. Add the oil, vinegar, salt and parsley. Serve at room temperature.

Serves 6 as a side dish or 12 as a tapa.

Eggs Scrambled With Mushrooms and Green Garlic
Huevos Revueltos Con Setas y Ajetes

While this dish might be served as a tapa or starter, it makes a good light supper dish. Green garlic shoots, which look like miniature spring onions, have an amazingly mild flavour. If they are not available, substitute leeks, very finely chopped. In Spain this dish is made with any one of several types of wild mushrooms, but you could use cultivated white mushrooms instead.

150 g /5 oz mushrooms (such as chanterelles, oyster mushrooms or boletus)
6-8 green garlic shoots or ½ leek
3 tablespoons olive oil
150 g /5 oz peeled, raw prawns (shrimp) (optional)
1 tablespoon water
5 eggs
salt and pepper
squares of fried bread

Cut away any woody parts of the mushrooms, rinse under running water and pat them dry on a kitchen towel. Slice the mushrooms. Trim off ends of garlic shoots and chop them. Heat the oil in a frying pan and sauté the mushrooms and garlic until softened. Add the prawns, if desired, when mushrooms are ready. Beat together the water, eggs and salt and pepper. Pour into the mushrooms and cook, stirring, until eggs are set creamy-soft. Serve immediately. As a tapa, spoon the eggs onto squares of fried bread.

Makes 6-8 tapas or 2-3 supper servings.

Mixed Vegetable Casserole
Menestra de Verduras

A Spanish meal rarely consists of meat, potatoes and two veg. Vegetables make their appearance in many salads, in first-course dishes and cooked with pulses for hearty potages. This vegetable casserole makes a good starter. It can be divided between individual baking dishes, each topped with an egg, and baked until the egg is set—a fine supper dish. Vegetarians can omit the ham from the mixture. While the following recipe is a typical spring menestra, you could use green beans, pumpkin, chard, carrots, cauliflower or other veggies, according to the season.

250 g /½ lb shelled peas
250 g /½ lb shelled broad beans (fava beans)
500 g /1 lb fresh artichokes, trimmed and quartered (or half that weight if using frozen artichoke hearts)
1 carrot, peeled and sliced
3 tablespoons olive oil
1 small onion, chopped
2 cloves garlic, chopped
1 tablespoon flour
salt and pepper
½ teaspoon paprika
6 tablespoons tomato sauce (recipe follows)
water or stock
parsley or mint to garnish

Partially cook each vegetable individually in boiling water to cover— peas, broad beans, artichokes and carrots. Drain, reserving some of the cooking liquid. In a heatproof earthenware casserole, heat the oil and sauté the chopped onion and garlic. Add the cooked and drained vegetables and sauté gently. Sprinkle with the flour, salt and pepper and paprika. Add the tomato sauce and reserved cooking liquid or stock. Cook on a medium heat until vegetables are very tender, about 20 minutes. Serve garnished with chopped parsley or mint.

Serves 12 as a tapa or 6 as a side dish.

bay leaf
sprig of parsley
100 ml /3 ½ fl oz (⅓ cup) water, white wine or stock

Sauté the chopped onion and garlic in the oil until the onion is softened. Add the tomatoes and fry on a hot fire for a few minutes. Add the salt, bay, parsley and liquid. Bring to a boil, then simmer 15-20 minutes, or until liquid is reduced. Sieve the sauce or purée it in a blender.

Makes about 750 ml/1 ¼ pints (3 cups) of sauce.

Spinach with Raisins and Pine Nuts
Espinacas con Pasas y Piñones

The best raisins of all are the sweet Málaga muscatel. However, you could use any type of raisin. Chard can be used in the recipe instead of the spinach.
This mixture also makes a good filling for tiny pasties (pastry turnovers). Use the pastry dough recipe for Fried Tuna Pasties (see recipe page 41).

1 ½ kg/3 lbs spinach or chard, washed, trimmed and
    chopped
3 tablespoons olive oil
50 g/1 ¾ oz (⅓ cup) pine nuts
2 cloves garlic, chopped
80 g/3 oz (½ cup) raisins, seeded
salt and pepper

In a large pan, heat the oil and fry the pine nuts just until they are golden. Skim them out and reserve. Add the chopped garlic and the spinach to the pan. Cook the spinach in the oil until wilted. Then add the raisins and salt and pepper and just a little water. Cover and cook the spinach 10 minutes. Stir the toasted pine nuts into the spinach and serve.

Tomato Sauce
Sofrito de Tomate

This is a basic sauce in Spanish cooking—the starting point for many different dishes. It doesn't require long simmering, because it usually will cook further with the vegetables, meat, poultry or whatever. If you like a really smooth sauce, the sofrito can be sieved or puréed in a blender.

1 small onion, chopped
1 clove garlic, chopped
4 tablespoons olive oil
2 kg/4 lbs tomatoes, peeled and chopped
1 teaspoon salt

Squid in Black Ink Sauce

Calamares en Su Tinta

This will be a sensation at your tapas party. It's exotic, but delicious, and not at all difficult to prepare. The black ink comes from a tiny sac inside the squid—or you can buy it in a sachet at the frozen-foods stand at markets in Spain. This dish is of Basque origin, but squid ink also goes into a Catalan dish of black rice.

1 kg/2 lbs small squid
100 g/3 ½ oz ham, chopped
30 g/1 oz (¼ cup) breadcrumbs
1 clove garlic, minced
2 tablespoons olive oil
450 ml/¾ pint (2 cups) tomato sauce
    (see recipe on page 28)
2 tablespoons brandy
pinch of cayenne
cooked short-grain white rice
chopped parsley

Your fishmonger will probably be willing to clean the squid for you—but be sure to reserve the ink sacs and leave the body pouch whole. Here's how to clean the squid yourself: pull the head, which has short tentacles attached to it, gently away from the body pouch. This releases the innards, to which is attached the silvery ink sac. Cut it away and reserve in a cup. Cut off the tentacles just above the eyes. Save the tentacles and discard the rest. Reach inside the pouch and free the quill, the transparent cartilage, and discard it. Wash the body pouch and pull off the dark-coloured skin covering it. This will free the fins. Save them. You're now ready to proceed with the recipe.

Chop the fins and tentacles. Combine them with the ham, breadcrumbs and minced garlic. Use this mixture to stuff the body pouches of the squid. Close the tops with toothpicks. Heat the oil in a frying pan or earthenware casserole big enough to hold the squid in one layer and sauté the squid gently. They don't need to brown. Add the tomato sauce, brandy and cayenne, plus salt and pepper to taste. Cook until the squid are very tender, about 25 minutes. Mash the ink sacs which you have set aside in a cup and dilute the ink with a little white wine or water. Pour into the sauce and cook another few minutes. (If you like the idea of serving the white squid atop black sauce, remove them before adding the ink to the sauce.) Press the cooked rice into a small oiled mould and unmould it onto an individual serving dish. Place one or two squid next to it and pool the sauce around them. Garnish with chopped parsley. To serve as small tapa portions, the squid can be sliced crosswise into bite-size pieces.

Makes 6 starters or 12 tapas.

Octopus, Galician-Style
Pulpo a la Gallega

If you can find frozen, cooked octopus, this is an easy dish to prepare. Otherwise, octopus needs an hour or more to simmer to become tender.

500 g/1 lb frozen, cooked octopus, thawed
2 large potatoes, boiled, peeled, and cut in chunks
coarse salt
chopped garlic (optional)
1 tablespoon paprika
100 ml/3 ½ fl oz (⅓ cup) olive oil

Use scissors to cut the cooked octopus into bite-size pieces. Place them on a dish (typically a wooden dish in Galicia) with chunks of the potato. Sprinkle with coarse salt, chopped garlic, paprika. Then drizzle over the oil. Serve at room temperature.

Makes 6 small tapa servings.

Clams, Fishermen's Style
Almejas a la Marinera

You will be amazed at the variety of shellfish to be found in Spanish tapa bars! Ten or more sorts—crustaceans and molluscs plus some odd ones, such as barnacles—each prepared in several different manners. Some of the best are the most simple, such as this way with clams—which, by the way, can be used with mussels as well.

Use any small steamer clam or wedge-shell clam. The big Venus-shell clams, with their beautiful polished shells, aren't suitable for this dish, as they toughen with cooking. They are more appropriately served raw on the half-shell.

This is a tapa frequently served from a communal platter. Go right ahead, dip your chunk of bread into the delicious, garlicky juice!

½ kg /1 lb small clams
1 tablespoon chopped onion
2 cloves chopped garlic
3 tablespoons olive oil
6 tablespoons white wine
6 tablespoons water
piece of chili pepper (optional)
1 bay leaf
2 tablespoons chopped parsley

Wash the clams in running water. Discard any which are opened or cracked. In a deep frying pan, fry the chopped onion and garlic in the oil for a few minutes until onion is softened. Add the clams. On a high heat, add the wine, water, chili and bay leaf. Cover and shake the pan vigorously until the clam shells open. This takes about 3-4 minutes. Remove from heat when most of shells have opened. Pour into a serving dish and top with chopped parsley. Serve with chunks of bread to dunk into the clam juices.

Serves 8 as a shared tapa, or 2 or 3 as a first course dish.

Mussels Vinaigrette
Mejillones a la Vinagreta

If you must buy the mussels before the day you intend to serve them, steam them open and refrigerate, covered with their juices. Once cooked, they keep for several days. Lemon juice is an excellent substitute for the vinegar in this recipe.

2 dozen + mussels
shredded lettuce
2 tablespoons minced onions
2 tablespoons minced green pepper
2 tablespoons minced red pepper
1 tablespoon chopped parsley
4 tablespoons olive oil
2 tablespoons vinegar

Scrub the mussels, chip off any barnacles, remove the beards (the sea-weedy tuft with which they attach themselves to rocks), and rinse in running water. Put them in a deep pan with just a little water. Cover and put over a hot fire. Shake the pan until the mussel shells open, two or three minutes, removing them from heat as soon as they open. Discard any which do not open. When the mussels have cooled, discard empty half-shell. Chill the mussels. Arrange them on a serving dish atop a bed of shredded lettuce. Combine the minced onions, green pepper, red pepper, parsley, oil and vinegar. Spoon the mixture onto the mussels in their shells.

Makes 24 tapas.

Scallop Gratin
Vieiras Gratinadas

Scallops are emblematic of Galicia, because the shells were an ancient symbol for those who made the pilgrimage to the shrine at Santiago de la Compostela. Fresh scallops include the collop of white muscle, plus the coral foot. Use frozen scallops if fresh ones are not available.

1 ½ dozen scallops in their shells (or equivalent frozen scallops)
3 tablespoons olive oil
1 small onion, minced
1 clove garlic, minced
30 g/1 oz ham or bacon, diced
2 tablespoons white wine
2 teaspoons paprika
salt and pepper
30 g/1 oz (¼ cup) fine breadcrumbs
1 tablespoon olive oil

If using fresh scallops, open the shells by inserting a knife between the shells and prising them open. Discard the empty flat shell. Loosen scallops from their shells. Cut out and discard the mantle and black sac. Rinse the scallops in running water. Clean the shells. Place one or two scallops in each shell and set them on a grill (broiler) pan. Heat the oil in a frying pan and sauté the minced onion, garlic and diced ham until onion is softened. Add the wine, paprika, salt and pepper. Spoon this mixture over the scallops in the shells. Combine the breadcrumbs with the oil and just a little water to make a paste. Spoon it on top of the scallops. Place the pan under the grill (broiler) until the tops are browned and scallops are bubbling, about 8 minutes.

Makes 6 starters or 18 individual tapas.

Marinated
Fresh Anchovies
Boquerones al Natural

So different is this dish from salty, tinned anchovies, that there should be another name entirely for this little fish. The tiny, fresh anchovies are filleted and marinated in vinegar to produce this tapa dish, which is found everywhere in Spain. If you can't get fresh anchovies, substitute thin strips of sardine, herring or mackerel.

½ kg /1 lb fresh anchovies
125 ml /4 fl oz (½ cup) wine vinegar
½ teaspoon salt
shredded lettuce, if desired
2 cloves garlic, coarsely chopped
2 tablespoons parsley, chopped
2 tablespoons olive oil
lemon juice

Cut off the heads and gut the fish. With a knife tip, grasp the top of the spine and pull it down across the belly to fillet the fish. Cut it off at the tail, leaving the two fillets attached by the tail. Rinse the fillets in cold water, then drain and place them in a single layer in a glass, ceramic or plastic dish. Add salt and enough vinegar to completely cover them. Cover and marinate for 24 hours or longer. The flesh will turn solid and white, cooked by the vinegar. Before serving, rinse the fish in ice-water and drain well. Arrange them on a plate, on a bed of shredded lettuce, skin side down, in spoke-fashion. Sprinkle with chopped garlic and parsley and drizzle with oil and just a touch of lemon juice. To serve the anchovies as canapés place them on strips of bread.

Makes 12 tapa servings.

Orange and Cod Salad
Remojón

The codfish used in this salad is *bacalao*, dry salt cod, which is immensely popular in Spain. If not available, you could substitute tinned tuna or well-rinsed tinned anchovies, chopped.

100 g / 3 ½ oz dry salt cod
4-6 oranges, peeled and sliced
1 onion, thinly sliced (red onion if possible)
1 clove garlic, crushed
4 tablespoons olive oil
1 tablespoon wine vinegar
a few red pepper flakes (optional)
20 green or black olives

Toast the salt cod over a flame or under the grill until it is lightly browned and softened. Put it in a bowl of water while preparing the remaining ingredients. Arrange the orange and onion slices on a plate. Whisk the garlic with the oil, vinegar and red pepper flakes. Drain the cod and remove all skin and bones. Shred it and add to the salad. Sprinkle the dressing over the salad and garnish with the olives.

Makes 12-14 tapa servings.

Hot Potatoes
Patatas Bravas

These potatoes are hot as in chili peppers, which go into the sauce.

For the brava sauce:
175 ml/6 fl oz (⅔ cup) tomato sauce
    (see recipe, page 28)
1 tablespoon olive oil
1 clove garlic, crushed
1 tablespoon vinegar
1 teaspoon paprika
½ teaspoon ground cumin
cayenne or red pepper flakes to make the sauce hot
salt

Combine the tomato sauce, oil, garlic, vinegar, paprika, cumin, cayenne and salt.

For the potatoes:
500 g / 1 lb potatoes, peeled and cut in
    3 cm/1 ¼ inch cubes
olive oil for frying
salt

Fry the cubed potatoes in deep hot oil until they are golden-brown and tender (test them by piercing with a skewer). Drain them on paper towelling and sprinkle with salt. Heap the potatoes on a platter and pour the sauce over them.

Makes 8 tapa servings.

Baked Eggs,
Flamenco Style
Huevos a lo Flamenco

olive oil
325 ml/11 fl oz (1 ⅓ cups) tomato sauce
    (see recipe on page 28)
100 g/3 ½ oz ham, chopped
8 eggs
2 tablespoons cooked peas
strips of tinned red pimiento
slices of chorizo sausage
8 asparagus tips
salt and pepper
chopped parsley

Oil four (or eight) individual oven-proof ramekins and divide the tomato sauce between them. Sprinkle a little chopped ham into each. Break one or two eggs into each ramekin. Sprinkle on a few cooked peas, criss-cross the top with strips of pimiento, and set a chorizo slice next to the eggs. Top with asparagus tips. Sprinkle with salt and pepper and chopped parsley. Bake in a medium-hot oven (200º C/ 400º F) until whites are set but yolks still liquid, about 8 minutes.

Makes 4 supper servings or 8 tapas.

Fried Squid Rings
Calamares Fritos

Clean the squid (see instructions in the recipe for Squid in Ink Sauce), discarding the innards and ink sac. Cut the body pouch crosswise into rings. The tentacles can be left in one piece or, if large, cut in half. Pat dry on a clean kitchen towel. Place the pieces in a bowl of plain flour and toss them to coat. Heat olive oil in a deep-fryer or deep frying pan. The oil should be about 180º C/ 350º F. Scoop the squid into a colander or flat-bottomed sieve and shake to eliminate excess flour. Fry the squid in the oil. Remove when golden. Drain on paper towelling, sprinkle with salt. Serve with lemon wedges.

3 or 4 rings make 1 tapa serving.

Prawns in Overcoats
Gambas en Gabardinas

500 g/1 lb raw jumbo prawns (shrimp),
    peeled, leaving the tails intact
1 egg, beaten
4 tablespoons water
½ teaspoon salt
¼ teaspoon bicarbonate of soda (baking soda)
100 g/3 ½ oz (¾ cup + 1 tablespoon) plain flour
olive oil for deep-frying

Combine the egg, water, salt, bicarbonate and flour to make a batter which is thick enough to coat the prawns. If necessary, thin with water, a few drops at a time. Heat the oil to 180º C/ 350º F. Dip the prawns by their tails into the batter then fry in the hot oil. The batter should puff slightly. Remove the prawns when golden. These are good served with a spicy tomato sauce (see the recipe for the sauce with Hot Potatoes page 37).

Makes about 10 tapa servings (allowing for 3 prawns per person).

Tuna Pasties
Empanadillas de Atún

For the dough:
270 g/9 ½ oz (2 ¼ cups) plain flour
1 teaspoon salt
100 g/3 ½ oz (½ cup + 1 tablespoon) butter or lard
100 ml/3 ½ fl oz (⅓ cup) white wine, chilled

Place the flour and salt in a bowl and cut in the butter or lard with a pastry cutter until crumbly. Add the cold wine. Press the dough together to form a ball. Wrap in cling film and refrigerate for at least two hours. (You can buy prepared rounds of empanadilla dough in the refrigerated section at big supermarkets in Spain.)

For the filling and frying:

200 g/7 oz tinned tuna, well drained
3 tablespoons tomato sauce
1 hard-boiled egg, chopped
1 tablespoon minced onion
1 tablespoon chopped parsley
1 tinned red pimiento, chopped
1 dozen pitted green olives
a few fennel or cumin seeds
salt and pepper
pinch of cayenne or dash of hot pepper sauce
olive oil for frying

Flake the tuna and combine in a bowl with the tomato sauce, chopped egg, onion, parsley, pimiento and olives. Season with fennel, salt and pepper and hot pepper sauce.

Roll out the chilled dough on a lightly floured board and cut it into rounds of approximately 10 cm/4 inches in diameter. Place a small spoonful of filling on each round and fold over the dough to make half-circles. Seal the edges with a fork. Heat the oil in a deep-fryer or deep frying pan to 180º C/ 350º F. Fry the pasties a few at a time until they are golden brown. Drain on paper towelling and serve hot. These pasties can be prepared in advance and then frozen. Freeze them in a single layer, then pack them in layers in a covered freezer container. Do not thaw, but remove from deep-freeze about 20 minutes before frying. Fry them without defrosting, but allow a longer time in the hot oil.

Makes 2 dozen pasties.

Chapter 2
Soups

Every region of Spain boasts super soups. Some are light and refreshing, like summertime gazpacho, made with raw ingredients. Others are heart-warming potages chock-full of pulses, vegetables, meat and sausage. Then there are dozens of fish and shellfish soups as well.

Cold Andalusian Tomato Soup
Gazpacho Andaluz

Gazpacho is simple peasant food, the sort of midday dish made in the fields, which requires only raw vegetables, bread, garlic and olive oil. Its goodness depends on big, juicy, vine-ripened tomatoes. In tapa bars gazpacho is often served in tall glasses, without the garnishes, to be sipped. On a hot summer's day, it really hits the spot.

75 g/2 ½ oz (3 slices) stale bread. Use Spanish, French or
    Italian loaf, not packaged sandwich bread
1 kg/2 lbs (4 large) ripe tomatoes
3 cloves garlic
2 teaspoons salt
6 tablespoons olive oil
5 tablespoons vinegar
approximately 300 ml/½ pint (1 ¼ cups) water

For the garnishes:
100 g/3 ½ oz green pepper (1 small pepper), finely
    chopped
200 g/7 oz cucumber (½ cucumber),
    peeled and finely chopped
1 small onion, finely chopped
1 small tomato, finely chopped
50 g/1 ¾ oz (2 slices) bread, diced and
fried crisp in a little olive oil

Put the bread to soak in enough water to cover for 10 minutes. Squeeze out excess water and discard crusts. Purée the tomatoes in a blender or processor, then sieve the pulp to remove all skin and seeds. Put the garlic in a blender or processor and whiz to chop finely. Add the bread, then the tomato pulp. (If necessary, process in two batches.) With the motor running, add the salt, then the oil in a slow stream, then the vinegar. The mixture will thicken and change colour as the oil emulsifies. Add a little of the water and transfer to a serving bowl or pitcher. Add additional water to desired consistency— gazpacho is usually as thick as pouring cream. Chill until serving time.

Arrange the garnishes in separate bowls and serve with the gazpacho. Each person adds the accompaniments to taste.

Serves 6.

Castillian Soup
Sopa Castellana

Spain has garlic soup the way France has onion soup. Almost a cult. Served in every region of the country. Wonderfully restorative. This one is typical of Madrid. It is frequently served in individual earthenware bowls, each with an egg poached in the hot soup. While usually served as a first course, with the egg added, it could be a simple supper dish.

6 tablespoons olive oil
6 cloves garlic, peeled and chopped
300 g/10 ½ oz (10-12 slices) stale bread, cut in strips
1 tablespoon paprika
pinch of cayenne (optional)
1 ¾ litres/3 pints (7 ½ cups) water or stock
2 teaspoons salt
6 eggs
chopped parsley

In a soup pot heat the oil and fry the chopped garlic and strips of bread until lightly golden. Stir in the paprika (and cayenne), then immediately add the water or stock and salt. Bring the soup to a boil, then simmer until the bread is mostly dissolved, about 15 minutes. Ladle the boiling soup into individual ovenproof soup bowls and break an egg into each. Place them in a preheated hot oven until the whites are set but yolks still liquid. Sprinkle each with a little chopped parsley.

Serves 6.

Garnished Broth
Sopa de Picadillo

The broth which remains after serving cocido, an elaborate boiled dinner (see the recipe on page 59), would be garnished with chopped ham and croutons to make a light evening meal. Cocido broth is very rich, with chicken, beef and ham boiled in it. The fresh mint sets off the aromas beautifully. If you haven't got real cocido broth, use any good chicken stock boiled with a piece of ham or unsmoked bacon.

Tiny cups of the cocido broth are served in tapa bars. And it's considered a hangover cure for the morning-after.

2 litres/4 pints (8 cups) chicken and ham broth
3 tablespoons olive oil
100 g/3 ½ oz (3-4 slices) bread, cut in dice
100 g/3 ½ oz serrano ham, chopped
2 hard-boiled eggs, chopped
4 tablespoons dry Sherry
cooked chick peas (garbanzos), optional
sprigs of mint

Heat the broth. (It may, if desired, be skimmed of fat.) In a frying pan heat the oil and fry the diced bread until golden. Remove and reserve. Immediately before serving add the ham, chopped egg, Sherry and fried bread. Ladle the broth into soup plates and garnish each with a sprig of mint.

Serves 6.

Cold White Garlic Soup With Grapes
Ajo Blanco con Uvas

This version of gazpacho, typical of Málaga, is made with finely ground almonds instead of tomatoes. The sweet muscatel grapes make a marvellous counterpoint to the tangy, garlicky soup. Unusual and very sophisticated.

200 g/7 oz (6-8 slices) stale bread, crusts removed
200 g/7 oz almonds (1 ½ cups), blanched and skinned
3 cloves garlic
150 ml/¼ pint (½ cup) extra virgin olive oil
5 tablespoons wine vinegar
2 teaspoons salt
water, approx 1 litre/2 pints (4 cups) to dilute
1 bunch muscatel grapes, seeded if desired

Soak the bread in water until softened. Grind the skinned almonds in a processor with the garlic. Squeeze out the bread and add to the processor with just enough water to make a smooth paste. With the motor running, add the oil, then the vinegar and salt. Add a little of the water, then pour the mixture into a tureen or pitcher and add enough additional water to make the soup the consistency of cream. The soup should be quite tangy, so add additional vinegar if needed. Chill the soup. Stir before serving into bowls each garnished with three or four grapes.

Serves 6.

Galician Soup
Caldo Gallego

This potage includes a kind of greens typical of Galicia, *grelos*, which are the stems and leaves of a sort of turnip. You could substitute turnip greens, chard, collards, spinach or cabbage.

250 g/½ lb large white beans, soaked overnight
meaty ham bone, or salt-cured pork ribs
    or a piece of fresh pork
meaty beef marrow bone
piece of salt pork fat
3 medium potatoes
1 kg/2 lbs greens, washed and chopped
1 teaspoon paprika
salt

Drain the soaked beans and put them to cook in a large pot in about 3 litres/5 ¼ pints (3 quarts) of water with the ham bone or pork, the beef bone and salt pork fat. When the beans are partially cooked, add the potatoes, peeled and cut in small chunks. In a separate pot of boiling water, blanch the greens for 3 minutes. This removes excess bitterness. Add them to the beans and potatoes and taste for salt. Dissolve paprika in a little of the soup and stir it in. Cook another 30 minutes until potatoes and greens are tender. To serve, cut meat off bones and discard bones.

Serves 8.

Chapter 3
Main Dishes

You can serve almost any dish as a tapa. For example, a whole cooked fish would be presented at a tapa bar, to be scooped up by spoonfuls in tapa-size servings. However, most of the following are best served as main dishes.

Asturian Casserole of Beans and Sausages
Fabada Asturiana

Asturias is in the north of Spain on the Bay of Biscay, where winters can be very chill. Beans bubbling in a clay pot are just the thing to ward off the cold and stick to the ribs. The Asturian *fabes* are like plump lima or butter beans.

500 g / 1 lb dried white beans, soaked overnight in water
150 g / 5 ¼ oz streaky bacon, in one piece
250 g / ½ lb salt-cured pork hock or ham (if using dry, cured ham, soak it overnight)
250 g / ½ lb red *chorizo* sausage (preferably smoked Asturian)
250 g / ½ lb black *morcilla* sausage (preferably smoked Asturian)
2 bay leaves
¼ teaspoon saffron, crumbled
salt and pepper to taste

Drain the beans and put them in an earthenware casserole. Blanch the bacon in boiling water for 3 minutes and drain. Tuck the bacon into the beans and cover them with water. Bring to a boil and skim. Add the ham hock, chorizo, morcilla and bay leaves. Bring to a boil and skim again. Add saffron, dissolved in a little liquid. Then cover and cook very slowly, about 1-2 hours, or until beans are very tender. Add cold water during cooking so beans are always just barely covered with liquid. Taste for salt and pepper. Don't stir the beans, which breaks them up, but shake the casserole from time to time. Let the fabada rest for 15 minutes before serving.

Serves 6.

Chicken in Almond Sauce
Pollo en Pepitoria

Almond trees blossom pale pink in late winter. The nuts, which are harvested in the early fall, are widely used in Spanish cooking. Almonds are the main ingredient in *turrón*, nougat candy, and marzipan, both popular at Christmas time. They also go into many savoury dishes such as this chicken fricassee.

1 large chicken or boiling fowl
   (2-3 kg / 4 ½-6 ½ lbs), jointed
salt and pepper
flour
5 tablespoons olive oil
40 g/1 ½ oz (⅓ cup) almonds, blanched and skinned
6 cloves garlic, peeled
50 g/1 ¾ oz (2 slices) bread, crusts removed
1 onion, chopped
1 clove
10 peppercorns
½ teaspoon saffron
1 teaspoon salt
1 tablespoon chopped parsley
140 ml/½ pint (⅔ cup) dry Sherry or white wine
250 ml/9 fl oz (1 cup) chicken broth
1 bay leaf
2 hard-cooked egg yolks
1 tablespoon slivered almonds,
fried in a little oil until golden

Rub the chicken pieces with salt and pepper, then dredge them with flour. Heat the oil in a frying pan and fry the almonds, 4 cloves of garlic and the bread slices until they are golden and skim out. In the same oil, brown the chicken pieces very slowly on both sides, adding the chopped onion. Remove the chicken to a flameproof casserole.

In a mortar, grind the clove, peppercorns and saffron with the salt. Add the fried garlic, the remaining 2 cloves of raw garlic, almonds and bread (this can be done in a blender or processor), then the parsley. Dilute this mixture with some of the wine and stir it into the chicken pieces. Add the remaining wine and broth. Bring to a boil, then simmer, covered, very gently until the chicken is tender (1-2 hours, depending on size of the chicken). Mash the egg yolks with a little of the liquid and stir it into the casserole to thicken the sauce. Serve the chicken garnished with the toasted slivered almonds and triangles of fried bread.

Serves 6.

Paella With Seafood
Paella Con Mariscos

Paella appears at tapa bars, to be scooped up by small servings of a spoonful.

There are many versions of paella, some of which contain no seafood at all. This version, with shellfish and chicken, is very popular. The typical paella pan, which is often used on a wood fire out of doors, is wide and flat—quite unwieldy on the kitchen hob. You might try using a deeper pan—a flat-bottomed wok works well—or your largest frying pan.

Spanish rice is a medium-short grain variety, not a long-grained pilaff style rice. It soaks up the flavours with which it cooks, but tends to be sticky if overcooked. If Spanish rice isn't on your supermarket shelf, look for Italian arborio rice, the sort used for risotto.

Saffron is an expensive spice. If you can, buy it in Spain, where it's grown. If you don't have real saffron, use a spoonful of paprika for flavour plus a few drops of yellow food colouring to get that wonderful sunny yellow colour. (No, don't use that other yellow spice, turmeric, because it has a strong, sharp flavour of its own, which doesn't jibe with Spanish flavours.)

1 dozen mussels, scrubbed and steamed open
500 g/1 lb large, uncooked prawns (jumbo shrimp)
6 tablespoons olive oil
1 kg/2 lbs chicken or rabbit, cut in small pieces
300 g/10 oz squid, cleaned and cut in rings
2 small green peppers, cut in squares
2 large tomatoes, peeled and chopped
2 cloves garlic, minced
100 g/3 ½ oz shelled peas or broad beans,
    green beans or quartered artichokes
    (par-boil beans or artichokes)

1 ½ litres/2 ½ pints (6 ½ cups) water or stock
500 g/1 lb (2 ½ cups) Spanish short-grain rice
½ teaspoon saffron (or more, for a bright yellow colour)
a few peppercorns, crushed, or
    freshly ground black pepper
2 teaspoons salt
1 tinned red pimiento, cut in strips
lemon for garnish

Discard the empty half-shells of the mussels. Strain the liquid and reserve it. Cook 6-8 unpeeled prawns in boiling water for 1 minute. Set them aside and add the liquid to the mussel liquid. Shell the remaining prawns.

Heat the oil in a paella pan or large frying pan (approx. 40 cm/16 inches). Fry the chicken pieces in the oil, then add the squid. Continue frying, adding next the green peppers, then the tomato, garlic and peas, beans or artichokes. Combine the reserved liquid and stock or water to make 1 ½ litres / 2 ½ pints (6 ½ cups). Add all but 1 cupful of the liquid to the paella. Crush the saffron in a mortar or in a teacup using the butt-end of a knife. Dissolve it in a little water or white wine and stir into the paella with the pepper and salt. Add the peeled prawns. When the liquid comes to a boil, add the rice and continue to cook on a high heat for 6-8 minutes. Then reduce the heat and continue to cook until rice is just barely tender, adding the additional liquid as needed, about 8-10 minutes more. Don't stir the rice, but shake the pan. Garnish the top with the reserved mussels, cooked prawns and strips of pimiento. Let the paella rest for 5 minutes before serving with lemon wedges.

Serves 6.

Basque Style Hake
Merluza a la Vasca

Hake is a delicious fish, which belongs to the cod family. This Basque-style preparation is sometimes called "hake in green sauce." Green with lots of chopped parsley.

1 ½ kg/3 lbs whole fresh hake, cut into crosswise steaks
salt
2 tablespoons flour
100 ml/3 ½ fl oz (1/3 cup) olive oil
6 cloves garlic, sliced crosswise
150 ml/¼ pint (⅔ cup) white wine
½ teaspoon salt
50 g/2 oz peas
150 g/5 oz clams
a few peeled prawns (shrimp), if desired
2 tablespoons chopped parsley
6 cooked or tinned asparagus spears

Salt the fresh fish steaks and let them sit for 15 minutes. Then pat dry and dust them with the flour. Heat the oil in a flameproof earthenware casserole or frying pan. Add the sliced garlic and the pieces of hake. Let them cook, without browning, in the oil for 2 minutes on each side. Then add the wine, salt, peas, clams and, if desired, a few prawns. Cook the fish, shaking and rocking the casserole, until the fish is just flaky and clam shells opened. The sauce should be somewhat thickened. Add the chopped parsley and asparagus.

Serves 6.

Seafood Casserole
Zarzuela de Pescados y Mariscos

Like the opera for which it is named, this seafood masterpiece deserves a dedicated audience. Only a full gala production number will do, so plan to buy three or four different fish, as many shellfish. Black tie optional.

4 servings each of 3 or 4 different kinds of fish, for example: monkfish, grouper, rockfish, rascasse, bream, hake, sea bass, conger; cut fish into cross-cut steaks or fillets
4 large prawns (jumbo shrimp), peeled, leaving the tails intact
4 Dublin Bay prawns (sea crayfish), whole, or a small lobster, quartered
2 dozen mussels, scrubbed and beards removed; steamed open (reserve liquid)
150 ml / ¼ pint (⅔ cup) olive oil
1 medium squid, cleaned and cut in rings
1 onion, chopped
4 tomatoes, peeled and chopped
3 tablespoons dry Sherry
3 tablespoons brandy
1 bay leaf
½ teaspoon saffron, crushed
2 cloves garlic
10 almonds, blanched, skinned and toasted
2 plain biscuits (cookies such as graham crackers) (*galletas* Marias)
150 ml / ¼ pint (⅔ cup) white wine
salt and pepper
dash of cayenne
chopped parsley

You will need a large frying pan in which to sauté the fish plus a heat-proof earthenware casserole to contain the seafood in one layer.

Salt the fresh fish lightly and set it aside. In a frying pan, heat half the oil and add to it the prepared squid and the chopped onion. Sauté until onion is softened, then add the prepared tomatoes and fry on a high heat for 5 minutes. Add the Sherry and brandy, plus just a little water. Cook on a medium heat until tomatoes are reduced, about 10 minutes. Put the sauce into the casserole.

Wipe out the frying pan and add some of the remaining oil. In it sauté the pieces of fish, turning them to seal both sides. They needn't brown. Remove them as fried and place onto the sauce in the casserole. Add oil to the frying pan as needed. Next sauté the prawns, Dublin Bay prawns or lobster and add to the casserole. Discard empty mussel shells and add the mussels to the casserole.

In a mortar or blender, grind together the bay leaf, crushed saffron, garlic, almonds and biscuits. Combine the wine with any reserved liquid from mussels and dilute the crushed spice mixture in some of the liquid. Add salt and pepper and cayenne. Add it and remaining liquid to the casserole. Place the casserole on top of the stove and cook until fish is just flaky, about 15 minutes. Shake the casserole, but don't stir. Serve garnished with chopped parsley.

Serves 4

Spanish Boiled Dinner
El Cocido Español

Spain's national dish, the *cocido*, is a whole meal in three acts with a sumptuous cast of ingredients. For feast days, it would be further enriched with a big meat dumpling. Left-over cocido broth can be used for *picadillo* soup (see recipe page 45).

250 g/½ lb chick peas, soaked overnight
400 g/14 oz boiling beef
100 g/3 ½ oz salt pork or streaky bacon
meaty ham bone
½ boiling fowl or large chicken
3-4 carrots, peeled
1 turnip, peeled and halved
2 leeks, trimmed
1 stalk celery
1 onion stuck with 2 cloves
2 teaspoons salt
6 medium potatoes
1 small cabbage
150 g/5 oz red *chorizo* sausage
150 g/5 oz black *morcilla* sausage
150 g/5 oz fine soup noodles
sprigs of parsley
tomato sauce, if desired, as an accompaniment

Drain the chick peas and place them in a large cooking pot. Add the boiling beef, salt pork, ham bone, and boiling fowl. Add 4 litres/4 quarts of water and bring to a boil. Skim off the froth, then lower the heat and add the carrots, turnip, celery, leeks and onion. Simmer very gently, covered, for 1 hour. Then add the salt and cook another 30 minutes. Separate about 1 ½ litres/1 ½ pints (6 cups) of the broth into another saucepan. In it cook the cabbage, cut into wedges, with the two sausages for 30 minutes. Add the potatoes to the main pot and continue cooking it for another 30 minutes. When meat and chick peas are very tender, strain out the broth into another pot. Bring to a boil and cook the noodles in it.

Serve the noodle soup as a first course, garnished with sprigs of parsley. Skim out cabbage onto a platter with the other vegetables and chickpeas. Serve meat, sausages and chicken on a third platter. If desired, serve a tomato sauce with the cocido.

Serves 6.

Herb-Marinated Pork Loin

Lomo en Adobo

You'll find this tasty pork loin served as a tapa, when it is thinly sliced and quickly fried, then served atop a piece of bread, called *montadito* or *planchita*. In this version, the whole loin is oven-roasted, then sliced. It makes a nice dish for a buffet supper, especially when accompanied by the following potato casserole and the Spinach with Pine Nuts and Raisins (recipe on page 28).

1 ½ kg/3 lbs boned pork loin
4 cloves garlic, crushed
1 teaspoon paprika
2 teaspoons oregano
pinch of thyme

pinch of rosemary
10 peppercorns
1 teaspoon salt
1 tablespoon olive oil
200 ml/7 fl oz (¾ cup) wine vinegar
    (preferably Sherry vinegar)

Rub the pork loin with the crushed garlic, paprika, oregano, thyme and rosemary. Place it in a non-reactive container. Sprinkle with the peppercorns, salt, and oil. Pour over the vinegar. Cover the container and marinate the pork, refrigerated, for two days. Turn the pork in the marinade twice a day. Drain the meat and pat it dry and place in a roasting pan. Put it in a hot oven (200º C/ 400º F) for 10 minutes to brown. Then reduce the heat to medium (180º C/ 350º F) and roast the pork until done. Test it after one hour—cut into the centre of the piece of meat. Meat should be juicy, only slightly pink in the centre. If still red, roast another 15-20 minutes. Allow the meat to rest for 10 minutes before slicing.

Makes 8 dinner servings or 2 dozen tapas.

Spanish Potato Casserole
Patatas a lo Pobre

The Spanish name, *a lo pobre*, means poor-man's style—a main dish of just potatoes. Nowadays, this casserole makes a great side dish with meat or fish.

2 kg/4 lbs potatoes
2 onions
2 small green peppers
1 tomato, sliced
150 ml/¼ pint (⅔ cup) olive oil
3 cloves garlic, chopped
3 tablespoons chopped parsley
2 bay leaves
½ teaspoon thyme
½ teaspoon paprika (or saffron)
100 ml/3 ½ fl oz (1/3 cup) white wine
100 ml/3 ½ fl oz (1/3 cup) water
salt and pepper

Peel the potatoes and slice them fairly thinly. Peel and slice the onions. Cut peppers in strips. Pour a little of the oil into the bottom of a flame-proof earthenware casserole or oven-safe pan. Arrange alternating layers of potatoes, onions, green peppers and tomato slices, sprinkling each layer with some of the chopped garlic and parsley. Break the bay leaves into pieces and tuck them among the potatoes with the thyme. Sprinkle with the paprika and pour over the remaining oil. Place the casserole on a medium heat just until potatoes start to sizzle. Add the wine and water. Season with salt and pepper. When the liquid comes to a boil, cover the casserole and put in a medium oven (180º C/350º F) until potatoes are tender, about 45 minutes. Let the casserole rest 10 minutes before serving.

Serves 10 as a side dish.

Lamb Braised With Sweet Peppers
Cordero al Chilindrón

This dish is from Aragón which grows wonderfully sweet peppers. The usual interpretation is lamb cut in chunks as for stew. In this version, tender little lamb chops are used.

1 kg/2 lbs lamb chops, trimmed of excess fat
salt and pepper
4 sweet red capsicum (bell) peppers
3 tablespoons olive oil
3 cloves garlic, chopped
150 g/5 oz serrano ham, cut in strips
1 small onion, chopped
3 large tomatoes, peeled and chopped

Rub the chops with salt and pepper. Roast the peppers under the grill (broiler) or over a gas flame, turning them until blistered and charred. Remove and let them rest, covered. Then peel them and cut the flesh into wide strips. Heat the oil in a flameproof casserole and brown the lamb chops on both sides. Add the chopped garlic, strips of ham, chopped onion and strips of pepper. Add the chopped tomatoes and cook briskly for 5 minutes. Then reduce heat and simmer until lamb is tender, about 20 minutes.

Serves 4.

Bull's Tail
(Braised Oxtail)
Rabo de Toro

The bullfighter whose art is most highly rated in the *plaza de toros* is awarded trophies for his performance—one ear, two ears, then the tail too for the most profound *faena*. You won't have to brave any fighting bulls to enjoy this dish, for butcher's oxtail works just fine. This slow-simmered dish produces a deep, rich gravy—good with potatoes or rice on the side.

1 whole oxtail, cut into crosswise pieces
3 tablespoons olive oil
1 onion, chopped
1 leek, chopped
3 carrots, diced
2 cloves garlic, chopped
50 g/2 oz serrano ham, chopped
5 tablespoons brandy
120 ml/4 fl oz dry Sherry or red wine
1 tomato, peeled and chopped
1 bay leaf
sprig of parsley
sprig of thyme
salt and freshly-ground black pepper
pinch of ground cloves
chopped parsley

Blanch the pieces of oxtail in boiling water for 5 minutes and drain. In a large pan or casserole, heat the oil and add the onion, leek, carrots, garlic and ham and sauté until onion is softened. Add the pieces of oxtail and brown them on a high heat. Add the brandy, set it alight, and stir until the flames die down. Then add the Sherry or red wine, chopped tomato, herbs, salt and pepper, cloves. Simmer until the meat is very tender, about 2 hours, adding additional liquid as needed. The sauce should be fairly thick. If necessary, thicken with a little flour whisked into the gravy. If desired, this dish can be prepared in advance, chilled, and excess fat skimmed off. This also allows flavours to mellow. Serve garnished with chopped parsley.

Serves 4.

Chapter 4
Sweets and Puddings

Many tapa bars double as cafés, where you can take coffee and sweet rolls in the mornings, before the hour for tapas arrives. And nowadays, many bars have restaurants where you can sit at a table and order a full meal—including a pudding. Here, then, is a sampling of Spanish sweets.

Anise-Scented Holiday Rings
Roscos de Navidad

Spain's version of the doughnut, scented with anise and cinnamon, is one of the favourite sweets at Christmas time. Typically, in regions which produce huge quantities of olive oil, they would be fried in this oil. You can substitute other vegetable oil.

200 ml/7 fl oz (¾ cup + 1 tablespoon) olive oil
3 tablespoons aniseed
zest of a small lemon, removed in 1 piece
180 g/6 1/3 oz (1 cup) sugar
200 ml/7 fl oz (¾ cup + 1 tablespoon) white wine
2 teaspoons cinnamon
1 kg/2 lbs 3 oz (7 1/2 cups) plain flour
2 eggs, separated
3 teaspoons bicarbonate of soda (baking soda)
oil for deep frying
140 g/5 oz (⅔ cup) sugar

Put the 200 ml/7 fl oz of oil in a frying pan and heat it with the piece of lemon peel. Add the aniseed and cook a few minutes just until the spice is fragrant. Remove and cool the oil. Skim out the lemon peel. In a bowl, combine the 180 g/6 ¾ oz of sugar with the wine, cinnamon and oil. Add 2 cups of the flour, then beat in the egg yolks and bicarbonate of soda. Beat the egg whites until stiff, then fold them into the batter. Gradually add the remaining flour, using the hands to work it in. The dough will be very sticky. Continue adding flour until it forms a soft dough which doesn't stick to the fingers. Take a small ball of the dough and roll it into a cord about 10 cm/4 inches long. Pinch the ends together to form a circle. Continue forming the rings. Heat oil in a deep fryer until hot but not smoking and fry the rings, a few at a time, until golden on both sides. Remove them with a skimmer, drain briefly, and, while still hot, dredge them in the remaining sugar.

Makes 6-7 dozen small rings.

Catalan Custard with Burnt Sugar Topping
Crema Catalana

6 egg yolks
150 g/5 ¼ oz (¾ cup) sugar
750 ml/1 pint 6 fl oz (3 ¼ cups) milk
zest of 1 lemon
6 cm/2 inches cinnamon stick
100 ml/3 ½ fl oz (¾ cup + 1 tablespoon) milk
3 tablespoons cornflour (cornstarch)
50 g/1 ¾ oz (¼ cup) sugar

In a bowl beat the egg yolks with the 150 g/5 ¼ oz sugar. Put the 750 ml/1 pint 6 fl oz milk in a pan with the lemon zest and cinnamon stick. Bring to a boil, then remove from heat. Strain it and whisk into the beaten yolks. Stir the remaining milk and cornflour together in a small bowl until smooth. Stir it into the custard mixture. Cook the custard on a low heat, stirring constantly, until it just begins to bubble. Remove from the heat and divide between 6 shallow pudding dishes. Cool the custard.

Shortly before serving, sprinkle the tops of the custards with the remaining sugar. Use a salamander, heated on a gas flame, to carmelize the top of each custard. Or, set the sugar-topped custards under a grill to brown the sugar.

Serves 6.

Santiago Almond Torte
Torta de Santiago

This torte comes from Santiago de Compostela in northern Spain, where the shrine of St. James (Santiago) is located. Sometimes the torte has the outline of the cross of St. James on its top.

500 g / 1 lb almonds, blanched, skinned and finely ground
150 g / 5 ¼ oz (⅔ cup) butter
500 g / 1 lb 2 oz (2 ¾ cups) sugar
7 eggs
150 g / 5 ¼ oz (1 ¼ cups) plain flour
1 tablespoon lemon zest
icing (confectioner's) sugar

Spread the ground almonds in an oven tin and toast them in a moderate oven, stirring frequently, until they are lightly golden. Take care they do not brown. Cool. Cream the butter and sugar until light and fluffy. Beat in the eggs one at a time, then stir in the flour, ground almonds and grated lemon zest. Pour into a buttered spring-form mould and bake in a preheated moderate oven (180º C / 350º F) until a skewer inserted in the centre comes out clean, about 1 hour. Cool the torte 10 minutes, then remove from the mould and cool on a rack. Before serving dust the top with icing sugar. If desired, place a template of the Santiago pilgrim's cross on the torte, sprinkle with sugar, brush sugar off the template and remove it.

Serves 10, cut in thin wedges. This torte is good served with fruit purées.

Spanish Sponge Cake
Bizcocho

8 eggs, separated
500 g/1 lb 2 oz (2 ⅔ cups) sugar
1 teaspoon grated lemon zest
250 g/8 ¾ oz (2 cups + 2 tablespoons) plain flour, sifted

Prepare a cake tin (28 cm / 11 inches). Oil the bottom and sides and line the bottom with an oiled piece of parchment (baking) paper.

Place the egg whites in a bowl and with an electric mixer, beat them until stiff. In a separate bowl, beat the yolks until light, then beat in the sugar and continue beating until yolks are pale and creamy. Add the lemon zest. Beat the yolk mixture into the whites. By hand, fold the flour lightly into the sponge. Pour the batter into the prepared cake tin and bake in a preheated medium (180º C / 350º F) oven until a skewer inserted in the centre comes out clean, about 45 minutes. Loosen the sides with a knife and invert the cake onto a rack to cool.

The cake can be split and filled with fruit preserves, pastry cream or whipped cream. Or, use it for "tipsy cakes".

Serves 10-12.

Tipsy Cakes
Borrachos

This is a good way to use stale sponge cake.

1 sponge cake (recipe precedes), baked in a square or
    rectangular pan
200 g/7 oz (¾ cup) sugar
200 ml/7 fl oz (¾ cup + 1 tablespoon) water
zest of 1 orange
200 ml/7 fl oz (¾ cup + 1 tablespoon) medium or
    amontillado Sherry
3 tablespoons brandy
almond flakes, candied cherries
whipped cream, if desired

Cut the sponge into squares. Place them on a tray and prick the sponge all over with a skewer. In a saucepan combine the sugar, water and orange zest. Bring to a boil and cook for 5 minutes. Remove from heat and add the Sherry and brandy. Spoon the syrup over the cake squares. Let the syrup soak in, then add any remaining syrup. Squares of the cake can be set into fluted paper cups and decorated with almond flakes and candied cherries. Or, on a dessert plate, serve them with a dollop of whipped cream and a few fresh berries.

Makes 2 dozen servings.

Fruit in Sweet Wine Syrup
Arrope

Traditionally, this was a way to preserve summer's fruits and vegetables in a heavy syrup. Delicious with any combination of late-summer fruits such as melon, figs, pears, apples, and vegetables too. Unusual though it sounds, chunks of pumpkin and aubergine go very well in the spicy syrup.

1 kg/2 lb firm pears (8-10)
300 g/10 oz pumpkin or other vegetables
a few dried figs
a handful of raisins
zest of 1 lemon, cut into slivers
100 g/3 1/2 oz (¾ cup + 1 tablespoon) sugar
3 cm/1 inch cinnamon stick
4 cloves
¼ teaspoon allspice
500 ml/¾ pint (2 ¼ cups) Málaga muscatel wine or
    grape juice
slivered almonds

Peel the pears, quarter them and remove cores. Peel the pumpkin and cut it into chunks. Combine them in a saucepan with the figs and raisins, slivered lemon zest, sugar, cinnamon, cloves, allspice and wine or grape juice. Bring to a boil, then simmer until fruits are tender, about 30 minutes. Serve hot or cold, sprinkled with slivered almonds.

Serves 12.

"Heavenly Bacon"
Tocino de Cielo

A slab of this dense, sweet custard, with its dark caramel top, looks remarkably like a slab of bacon. Heavenly.

For the caramel:
200 g/7 oz (1 cup + 1 tablespoon) sugar
150 ml/¼ pint (5 fl oz) water

For the custard:
12 egg yolks
250 g/9 oz (1 ⅓ cups) sugar
400 ml/14 fl oz (1 ⅔ cups) water
1 piece of vanilla pod (bean)

First prepare the caramel. Have ready an oven-proof mould measuring approximately 16 x 16 cm/ 7 x 7 inches. In a heavy saucepan, boil the sugar and water until golden. Watching it very carefully, cook a little longer to a caramel colour. Immediately pour the caramel into the mould. Tip the mould to coat it evenly. Set aside while preparing the custard mixture.

Beat the yolks together until light and pass them through a fine sieve. In a heavy saucepan, heat the sugar with the water and vanilla pod. Cover for a few minutes, then uncover and boil the syrup to the thread stage, 10-15 minutes. A drop of the syrup, cooled, will spin a thread off the tip of a spoon. Remove the vanilla pod and whisk the hot syrup into the beaten egg yolks. Pour the mixture into the caramel-coated mould. Cover with foil and place the mould in an oven-proof pan. Partially fill the pan with boiling water. Set in a medium-low (150º C / 300º F) oven until the custard is cooked, about 25 minutes or when a thin skewer comes out clean. Cool the custard, then chill it. Turn the custard out of the mould and cut it into small squares or rectangles.

Makes 8-10 small pieces.

Creamy Rice Pudding
With Cinnamon
Arroz Con Leche

Rather better than the nursery pudding you remember. It's a favourite dessert amongst Spain's yuppies and politicos. Perhaps for the comfort value.

200 g/7 oz (1 cup) short-grain (pudding) rice
250 ml/9 fl oz (1 cup) water
1 piece cinnamon stick
strip of lemon zest
100 g/3 ½ oz (½ cup) sugar
pinch of salt
1 ¼ litres/2 pints (5 ¼ cups) milk
additional sugar
ground cinnamon

Put the rice and water to cook in a saucepan. Bring to a boil, cover and simmer just until the water is absorbed, about 6 minutes. Add the cinnamon stick, lemon zest, sugar, salt and milk. Bring to a boil, then turn the heat to very low and cook, covered, until the rice is tender, another 20 minutes. Remove the cinnamon stick and lemon peel. While the pudding is still hot, spoon it into a serving bowl or individual pudding dishes. Sprinkle with additional sugar and dust thickly with cinnamon. Cool. The pudding should still be creamy, not set too firm.

Makes 6-8 servings.

Sweet Fritters
Buñuelos

These puffed fritters have to be enjoyed freshly made. They are quite delicious accompanied by fruit jam, for breakfast or for dessert.

240 ml/8 ½ fl oz (1 cup) milk or water
70 g/2 ½ oz (⅓ cup) butter
30 g/1 oz (2 tablespoons) sugar
pinch of salt
125 g/4 ½ oz (1 cup) plain flour
4 eggs, room temperature
olive oil for deep frying the fritters
sugar

Place the milk or water, butter, sugar and salt in a saucepan and bring to a boil. Add the flour all at once, beating it hard with a wooden spoon. As you continue beating, it will form a smooth ball of dough. Remove from the heat and beat in the eggs, one at a time, until each is incorporated. Continue beating the batter until cool. (Batter can be prepared in advance.) Heat the oil in a deep-fryer or heavy frying pan. Drop the batter into the hot oil by spoonfuls. The batter will puff as it fries. Turn the fritters to brown both sides. Remove, drain and sprinkle the fritters with sugar.

Makes 2 dozen fritters.

Glossary

About Spanish Ingredients and Utensils

Anchovies (*boquerones, anchoas*). Fresh anchovies are small silvery fish— very different from salty tinned ones— which can be prepared in many ways. If not available in markets abroad, strips of fresh sardines, herring or mackerel might be substituted.

Casserole (*cazuela*). Earthenware casseroles with unglazed bottoms can be used for cooking on a gas hob or in the oven. If not available, use any flameproof casserole or frying pan. Earthenware holds the heat after it has been removed from heat, so food continues to cook.

Chorizo. Spain's most distinctive sausage. It is coloured red with paprika and flavoured with garlic. There are two types of chorizo—a hard-cured sausage, which is sliced and served as cold cuts—and a soft sausage, usually tied in links, which can be fried or added to potages.

Cod, dry salt codfish (*bacalao*). A favourite ingredient everywhere in Spain. The salt-cod must be soaked for 36 hours in several changes of water before being prepared. (An exception is the recipe in this book for salad with oranges, where the cod is merely toasted.)

Ham (*jamón*). In Spain ham usually means serrano ham. This is a salt-cured ham (not smoked), which is served raw, very thinly sliced, as a tapa or aperitif. It is also used in cooked dishes. Prosciutto or Parma ham is the closest substitute, though unsmoked gammon or back bacon could be used in cooked dishes. Serrano ham, if made from the small, brown Iberian pig which fattens on acorns, is labeled *iberico*, and is sometimes also called *pata negra*, which means black hoof. It is enormously popular, thus very expensive. Ordinary cooked ham, the sort you might use for a ham sandwich, is *jamón cocido*.

79

Morcilla. A black sausage made from pig's blood and seasoned with cinnamon, cloves, nutmeg, fennel, sometimes pine nuts or onions. It is stewed with pulses and vegetables in typcial potages.

Olive oil (*aceite de oliva*). Olive oil is good for you. Spanish olive oil is superb—the essential flavour in many dishes. There are three types of olive oil. The first and finest is extra virgin, the oil extracted from recently picked olives which have been crushed and cold-pressed. Because it is expensive, choose it for flavour—in salad dressings and marinades, in place of butter for dressing vegetables, drizzled over grilled fish. Next is virgin olive oil. It has a higher level of oleic acid and is usually somewhat stronger in flavour than the extra virgin. It is perfect for deep-frying—potatoes, fish, fritters. The third type is simply labeled olive oil. This is oil which has been refined (as all other oils are refined), then mixed with some virgin oil to restore the olive oil flavour. It is the least expensive and can be used as you would use any other vegetable oil.

Paella, paella pan (*paella*). This rice dish is named for the pan in which it cooks, a wide, flat pan which allows all the ingredients to cook in a single layer over a fast-burning fire or, nowadays, on a large gas ring. A paella pan large enough to serve 8 people (40 cm/15-16 inches) is hard to manage on a hob, though you can try placing it over two burners. Easier, make two paellas or else use a deeper pan. The pans are sold in hardware stores and supermarkets all over Spain. They are usually made of rolled steel, which rusts. After use, scour the pan and dry very thoroughly before storing. If you wish to keep left-over paella, store it refrigerated in a covered container and reheat in a microwave.

Peppers, capsicums; paprika (*pimientos; pimentón*). Spanish markets proffer a number of different sorts of capsicum peppers—huge bell peppers in green, red and yellow; crinkly, skinny green ones with a crisp taste; small piquant-sweet red *piquillo* peppers, which are usually peeled and canned; tiny green Padrón peppers for frying; dried sweet red peppers, such as *ñoras* and *choriceros*, which are used to flavour chorizo sausage. Several sorts of chili peppers can be found too, most fairly mild. Chili is not widely used in Spanish cooking. Paprika, a spice made by grinding red peppers, can be sweet or piquant. The finest Spanish paprika is made by drying peppers in wood smoke.

Rice (*arroz*). Use medium-short grain rice, not pilaff rice, for Spanish rice dishes. It does not need washing before cooking. Spanish rice needs careful monitoring while it cooks, as overcooked, it turns mushy. Remove from heat source when it is still slightly al dente and allow to rest five minutes to finish cooking from residual heat. Actual cooking time varies considerably, depending on what type of pan and quantities of liquid used. So, for example, rice in a paella pan cooks more quickly than in an earthenware cazuela.

Saffron (*azafrán*). This costly spice is grown in several regions of Spain. The spice, wispy threads of a deep orange colour, should be crushed (with a mortar and pestle, or in a teacup with the butt-end of a knife), then dissolved in a little liquid before adding to the food to be cooked. If real saffron is not available, use instead a spoonful of paprika and/or a few drops of yellow food colouring.

Vinegar (*vinagre*). Wine vinegar is used in Spanish cooking. There are some special ones—red wine vinegar from Rioja, Sherry vinegar from Jerez, and *cava* vinegar from Catalonia.

Wine (*vino*). Wines used in cooking include red (*tinto*), white (*blanco*), rosé (*rosado*), sparkling (*cava*), dry Sherry (*vino fino de Jerez*), medium Sherry (*vino oloroso* or *amontillado de Jerez*) and sweet Málaga wine (*vino moscatel de Málaga*).

Index of Recipes